FROGS II

FROGS II

• *More* sparkling resources for speakers

Stephen Gaukroger
& Nick Mercer

Scripture Union
130 City Road, London EC1V 2NJ

© Stephen Gaukroger and Nick Mercer 1993

The right of Stephen Gaukroger and Nick Mercer to be identified
as authors of this work has been asserted by them in accordance
with the Copyright, Designs and Patents Act 1988.

First published 1993
by Scripture Union, 130 City Road, London EC1V 2NJ

ISBN 0 86201 871 4

British Library Cataloguing in Publication Data
A catalogue record for this book is available from the
British Library.

Extract from *The Cocktail Party* by TS Eliot is reproduced with the
kind permission of Faber & Faber Ltd.

Extract from *The Velveteen Rabbit* by Margery Williams is reproduced
with the kind permission of William Heinemann Ltd.

Cartoons by Taffy

Phototypeset by Intype, London
Printed and bound in Great Britain by
Cox and Wyman Ltd, Reading

CONTENTS

ACKNOWLEDGEMENTS

We gratefully acknowledge the many speakers – good, bad and indifferent – which it has been our pleasure to listen to over the years. Especially those who know how to tell a story.

THE ART
OF
STORYTELLING

'Tell us a story!' Children have cried this to adults in every culture since language began. And for the grown-ups, the soap operas continue to pull the largest audiences. Much of the Bible came to us by way of story-telling. Parents told children the great stories of God's dealings with his people; they learned them by heart and told them to their children. Other stories were written with great care and stylistic purpose, like Jonah and Job, Ruth and Esther, but written primarily for reading out loud and remembering. The Bible was never penned as a modern study text; it was set down to be proclaimed by the leaders and acted on by all as it penetrated the heart and mind.

This is why Jesus told stories: those memorable parables and word pictures, stories about the Good Shepherd, and the Vine and so much that many Christians can still recite from memory.

There is a power in story telling that goes beyond the words themselves. When you play with computers, you are sometimes aware that there is a language behind the language that you type onto the screen – it is called a 'deep-level' language, and there are even deeper levels behind that language. In the same way, stories communicate at a level that is much deeper than the mere logic and syntax of the sentences. There is a deep mystery behind words, just as Jesus, the Word, is embedded at the heart of the mystery of the Trinity. Many preachers fail to appreciate this, and deliver the word of God in a framework worthy of an EC agricultural regulation. In a way, all preaching is – or should be – storytelling.

Stories can transport us to another realm, whether it is Revelation's Christ in glory, or Adam's brush with the angel of the flaming sword, or Joseph's many-coloured coat; and there, amazingly, they can reshape our lives.

Stories can often bring out old truths in new ways. This has been the success of *Peanuts* or *The Little Prince*, or *Jonathan Livingstone Seagull*, or that children's classic, *The Velveteen Rabbit*. Margery Williams is only restating a biblical truth but, because she says it in a different way, it comes across with fresh power:

> The Skin Horse had lived longer in the nursery than any others. He was so old that his brown coat was bald in patches and showed the seams underneath, and most of the hairs in his tail had been pulled out to string bead necklaces. He was wise, for he had seen a long succession of mechanical toys arrive to boast and swagger, and by-and-by break their mainsprings and pass away, and he knew that they were only toys, and would never

turn into anything else. For nursery magic is very strange and wonderful, and only those playthings that are old and wise and experienced like the Skin Horse understand all about it.

'What is REAL?' asked the Rabbit one day, when they were lying side by side near the nursery fender, before Nana came to tidy the room. 'Does it mean having things that buzz inside you and a stick-out handle?'

'Real isn't how you are made,' said the Skin Horse. 'It's a thing that happens to you. When a child loves you for a long, long time, not just to play with, but REALLY loves you, then you become Real.'

'Does it hurt?' asked the Rabbit.

'Sometimes,' said the Skin Horse, for he was always truthful. 'When you are Real you don't mind being hurt.'

'Does it happen all at once, like being wound up,' he asked, 'or bit by bit?'

'It doesn't happen all at once,' said the Skin Horse. 'You become. It takes a long time. That's why it doesn't often happen to people who break easily, or have sharp edges, or who have to be carefully kept. Generally, by the time you are Real, most of your hair has been loved off, and your eyes drop out and you get loose in the joints and very shabby. But these things don't matter at all, because once you are Real you can't be ugly, except to people who don't understand.'

(From *The Velveteen Rabbit*, Margery Williams, Heinemann 1989)

Hints for Storytellers

- Be utterly convinced of what you are saying. Act as if the fiction were a reality. If you've ever been to Disney World you will know that all those people dressed as Mickey Mouse or Donald Duck or Snow White, will never break the pretence, whatever you say to them. That is what makes the place so enchanting. Never apologise for the story or feel 'silly' while you are reading it.

- Never be bored by the material, however familiar it is to you.

- In a culture that is not very well tuned to poetry and myth, I usually give some words of explanation beforehand in order to help people know what they are looking for. I was amazed, speaking with a student who had read CS Lewis's *The Lion, The Witch and The Wardrobe*, when I realised he had not grasped any of the Christian imagery in the story.

- Learn by heart the opening and the ending and, if possible, the middle!

- Use regional accents or other voices, if you can do it convincingly and if it helps the storytelling. Peter Cotterell puts on an East End accent for his poem, *The Way To Up Is Down:*

I was dreaming, I suppose, and yet me dream was very odd
'Cos I thought I saw the angels standing round the throne of God.
Each one wore a crown of gold and sang like fifty choirs in one

And I felt I'd like to join them when me life on earth
   was done.

Course, I couldn't be an angel, but perhaps I'd find a
   place
Where I'd always hear the angels and just sometimes
   see God's face.
If I sat beside the choir I'd be no trouble on me own
And it really would be heaven to see God upon 'is
   throne.

It was just a simple question that I asked the angel
   host,
'Which way is the way to heaven? That's what worries
   me the most.'
You'd expect a simple answer from an angel with a
   crown,
But he said, 'There's only one way, and the way to up
   is down.'

Well, I didn't understand it, so I asked 'im once
   again,
'Be an angel, mate, and tell me which way's best for
   sinful men?'
But the angel choir turned round as one, and with one
   joyful shout
They replied: 'The way to up is down and the way to
   in is out.'

I tried again, I thought maybe they didn't understand:
' 'Ere mates, what is the way to God and to the Prom-
   ised Land?'
Then the angel boss stood out and whispered to me,
   soft as breath:

'The way to up is down, lad, and the way to life is death.

If you save your life you'll lose it', I could hear the angel say,
'If you think you see, you're blind, but if you ask to see, you may.
He who thinks he's fit for heav'n is on the downward path to hell,
For the poor man shall be rich and soon the sick man shall be well.'

Then the angels gathered round and sang the song I can't forget;
Though I haven't understood it, I shall understand it yet:
'God's ways aren't the same as your ways and his thoughts are different too,
For the way to up was down for Christ, and the way is down for you.'

● Body language is still very important, even if you are reading from a script. Use your hands and eyes to draw people into the story.

● Use appropriate background music occasionally: classical guitar music or a good musician, but not playing Christian songs – this is a distraction which encourages people to 'sing along' in their minds. I once read the Seven Trumpets of the Apocalypse from the Book of Revelation to impromptu accompaniment by a professional pianist. It brought home the mystery and awe of those obscure verses in a startling way.

• Find gifted people who can tell stories better than you. The change in voice can increase the impact. I can still remember a school teacher who learnt and recited TS Eliot's *Journey of the Magi*, and when he got to the end of the last stanza there was a stunned silence.

Hints for Storywriters

• Impromptu stories are usually poor and muddled unless you are a really accomplished raconteur. The best off-the-cuff comments are always carefully premeditated!

• Listen to good storytellers. There are plenty on the radio and many tapes available that you can listen to in the car. Garrison Keillor (Lake Woebegone) is a master writer and storyteller, bringing simple truths home from people's everyday lives.

• Remember that most short stories or poems, like Jesus' parables, make only one main point. The gruesome children's stories of the Brothers Grimm follow this rule, and so does any episode of *The Waltons*. Don't get sidetracked by obfuscatory secondary points!

• When possible, develop your own style and use recurring themes and catchphrases: 'Once upon a time. . .' 'And they all lived happily ever after . . .' 'It has been a quiet week in Lake Woebegone. . .' 'Truly, truly I say to you, the kingdom of heaven is like. . .' I started all my children's talks in one church with the sing-song liturgy 'Good morning children.' 'Good morning Mr Mer-cer.'

• Try writing your own parables to bring out afresh some of the startling twists in familiar Bible parables or passages. The original hearers of the story of the Pharisee and the Tax-collector thought the Pharisee was the goody. But we all know he's the baddy as soon as the story starts. And the title 'The Good Samaritan' gives the game away right from the start. For Jesus' audience, a good Samaritan was a contradiction in terms!

The Creator has made us creative beings – in his own image. Storytelling is a way to create and recreate, and through the Spirit's mysterious working to help shape people's lives to the truth of the Gospel, the Greatest Story ever told.

'. . . stories are the real life changers, for they *do* produce. Their first and most significant product is conversion. They also confront and change lives. They motivate to holiness, to prayer, and to a loving and continuing affair with Scripture' (From Calvin Miller, *Spirit, Word, And Story*, Word, 1989).

THE A-Z

of

stories,

illustrations,

anecdotes,

witticisms,

etc . . .

Abilities – hitherto undiscovered

A motorist who drove his Reliant Robin three-wheeler on the M20 at 105 miles per hour was fined £150 for speeding and banned from driving for twenty-one days. Magistrates at West Malling, Kent, heard that police following the driver were so amazed that they had the speedometer of their patrol car tested. The driver, a labourer, who was also ordered to pay £80 costs, said after the hearing that he bought the V-registration Reliant for £500, and 'would not change it for anything.'

Age

Growing old isn't so bad when you consider the alternative.

Maurice Chevalier

Alive again!

A pastor's son was driving through the bush to Uige when UNITA soldiers forced him to take them with him. He protested that the brakes on the vehicle were no good. They disbelieved him until they came to a steep hill. The soldiers jumped out as did the driver, who then hid in the long grass. The jeep crashed at the bottom of the hill and the soldiers set fire to it.

People saw it and word got to the pastor in Luanda that his son had been killed. So in the church they held a funeral thanksgiving service for him – but the son turned up in the middle of it. 'This my son was dead and is alive again!'

Appearances (which can be deceptive)

A bishop, the 'Brain of Britain' and a student were travelling together on a small plane. Suddenly, the captain announced that the plane was ditching and told the passengers to bail out – apologising that there were only two parachutes between the three of them. Immediately, the Brain of Britain grabbed one and jumped out. The student seemed remarkably unperturbed but, nevertheless, the bishop told him that, as he was old and prepared to meet his God, the student should take the other parachute. And then he asked him, 'How come you're so calm, anyway?' And the student replied, 'Well, the Brain of Britain just jumped out with my rucksack!'

21

Atheism

To you I'm an atheist. To God I'm the loyal opposition.

Woody Allen

Attitude

A German group of psychologists, physicians and insurance companies who co-operated on a research project designed to find the secret to long life and success, made a surprising discovery. The secret? Kiss your spouse each morning when you leave for work!

The meticulous German researchers discovered that men who kiss their wives every morning have fewer car accidents on their way to work than men who omit the morning kiss. The good-morning kissers miss less work because of sickness, and earn twenty to thirty per cent more money than non-kissers. How do they explain their findings? According to West Germany's Dr Arthur Szabo, 'A husband who kisses his wife every morning begins the day with a positive attitude.'

Authority

The Captain on the bridge of a large naval ship saw a light ahead, set for collision with his vessel. He signalled to it: 'Alter your course ten degrees south.' The reply came back: 'Alter *your* course ten degrees north.'

The Captain then signalled: 'Alter your course ten degrees south. I am a Captain.' The reply came back: 'Alter your course ten degrees north. I am a Seaman third-class.'

The Captain, furious by now, signalled back: 'Alter your course ten degrees south. I am a battleship!' The reply: 'Alter your course ten degrees north. I am a lighthouse.'

Baptism

There was the Baptist minister who at his first baptism became stagestruck. Standing in the pool with the candidate, he suffered a complete lapse of memory. He became so muddled that he forgot which sacrament he was administering. Eyes heavenward, he commanded: 'Drink ye all of it!'

Baptists

Billy Graham is sitting quietly in a restaurant one day when a hold-up man comes in brandishing a gun. 'Okay. I want everyone to file past me and hand me their wallets.' When Billy Graham arrives in front of the robber, the man recognises him and motions the evangelist to put his wallet back in his pocket. 'Put it away, Billy,' he says. 'We Baptists must stick together!'

The Bible

Every Christian must refer always and everywhere to the Scriptures for all his choices, becoming like a child before it, seeking in it the most effective remedy against all his various weaknesses, and not daring to take a step without being illuminated by the divine rays of those words.

Pope John Paul II

Complete Bibles in 322 languages   The number of languages into which at least one book of the Bible has been translated rose from 1,946 in 1990 to 1,978 in 1991, according to the United Bible Societies. In 1991, thirty-two languages received at least one book of the Bible for the first time, the largest first-time number since 1987. Complete Bibles were made available in four languages for the first time: two in Zaire, one in Guatemala, and one in Yugoslavia. That, as at the end of 1991, increases the number of languages with complete Bibles to 322.

American Bible Society figures
quoted in 'Christianity Today,' 6 April 1992

Bible study

'We'll carry on discussing it over cake and coffee, then at 9.00pm we'll have some feedback. . .'

The story is told of a South Sea Islander who proudly displayed his Bible to a GI during World War II. Rather disdainfully, the soldier commented, 'We've grown out of that sort of thing.' The Islander smiled and said, 'It's a good thing we haven't. If it weren't for this book, you'd have been a meal by now!'

'Is there a version in Vulcan yet?'

Books

A man goes into the cinema and buys a ticket for himself and his dog. The usher is amazed to see the dog laughing throughout the film. After the show she comments to the man as he leaves, 'I was staggered to see your dog laughing at the film!' The man replies, 'So was I. He hated the book!'

Calling

As long as God gives me breath, I expect to preach the Gospel!

Billy Graham

The issue for me is not whether women should be in ministry . . . The issue is whether those in ministry, women or men, have been called by God to be there!

Anne Graham Lotz

There is no work better than another to please God; to pour water, to wash dishes, to be a cobbler, or an apostle: all is one.

William Tyndale

God buries his workmen but carries on his work.

Charles Wesley

While women weep, as they do now, I'll fight; while little children go hungry, I'll fight; while men go to prison, in and out, as they do now, I'll fight; while there is a drunkard left, while there is a poor, lost girl upon the streets, where there remains one dark soul without the light of God – I'll fight! I'll fight to the very end!

William Booth

Calvary

Calvary is a telescope through which we look into the long vista of eternity and see the love of God breaking forth into time.

Martin Luther King, Jr

Change

A Ghanaian newspaper is reputed to have recorded the following piece of news: 'Ghana is to change over to driving on the right. The change will be made gradually.'

One minister to another at a fraternal: 'I can't stand change, especially in the collection!'

I have examined myself thoroughly and have come to the conclusion that I do not need to change much.

Sigmund Freud

Character

The way to gain a good reputation is to endeavour to be what you desire to appear.

Socrates

It is right to be contented with what we have, never with what we are.

Sir James Mackintosh

Children

The learned teach the child; the wise listen to him.

Church

The frenzied activities of evangelical Christians have become legendary. Thankfully, someone has now revised the old nursery rhyme so that it fits today's picture:

> Mary had a little lamb,
> 'Twas given her to keep,
> But then it joined the Baptist Church
> And died for lack of sleep.

Church growth

Could it be that just a few church members are like Pat the Irishman . . .?

Two Irishmen on a tandem eventually arrived, perspiring, at the top of a long hill.

'That was a stiff climb, Pat,' said one.

'It was that,' said Pat, 'and if I hadn't kept the brake on we would have gone backwards for sure.'

Circumstances

Adverse circumstances are like a feather bed: all right if you're on top!

Commitment

I don't mind if my life goes in the service of the nation. If I die today every drop of my blood will invigorate the nation.

> *Indira Gandhi, the night before she was assassinated by Sikh militants, 30 October 1984*

We know what happens to people who stay in the middle of the road: they get run over.

> *Aneurin Bevan*

Seen on an American car bumper: 'If you love Jesus, tithe! Any fool can honk!'

A group of clergymen were discussing whether or not they ought to invite Dwight L Moody to their city. The success of the famed evangelist was brought to the attention of the men.

One unimpressed minister commented, 'Does Mr Moody have a monopoly on the Holy Ghost?'

Another man quietly replied, 'No, but the Holy Ghost seems to have a monopoly on Mr Moody.'

Communication

The Revd W A Spooner, the English scholar who died in 1930, was reputed to have had a dreadful habit of confusing his message in the process of giving it:

On one occasion he announced to his congregation that the next hymn would be, 'From Iceland's greasy mountains.'

At a wedding he told the groom, 'It is kistomary to cuss the bride.'

Calling on the dean of Christ Church he asked the secretary, 'Is the bean dizzy?'

Giving the eulogy at a clergyman's funeral, he praised his departed colleague as a 'shoving leopard to his flock.'

In a sermon he warned his congregation, 'There is no peace in a home where a dinner swells', meaning, of course, 'where a sinner dwells.'

Speaking to a group of farmers, Spooner intended to greet them as 'sons of toil,' but what came out was, 'I see before me tons of soil.'

A sign in three languages in the Swiss village of Chateau d'Oex shows the impossibility of arriving at common European standards. In English, it says, 'Please do not pick the flowers.' In German: 'It is forbidden to pick the flowers.' In French: 'Those who love the mountains, leave them their flowers.'

The Times, 4 June 1992

'It's very nice, but did we really need stone cladding?!'

In seventeenth-century England, the Church was an important part of family life. In the small villages, the minister was personally acquainted with every member of his congregation and with their problems.

So it was natural that, one Sunday in Shropshire, Mrs Whitfield wanted her pastor to mention Mr Whitfield in the morning's prayers. Her husband had joined the Navy and was presently serving His Majesty, the King.

The lady sent a handwritten message to the pulpit: 'Timothy Whitfield, having gone to sea, his wife desires the prayers of the congregation for his safety.'

The ageing preacher, however, had trouble reading the scrawled note. Without thinking, he quickly pronounced: 'Timothy Whitfield, having gone to see his wife, desires the prayers of the congregation for his safety.'

The England Winger carefully explained to the rest of his rugby team that in a line-out he will shout a name beginning with 'e' if it's a short ball, and a name beginning with 'o' if it's a long ball. At the first line-out the team heard him shouting, 'Oedipus!'

A young man was about to be married, but it wasn't until the night before the wedding that he tried on his suit. The rest of the family were horrified to see that the trousers were three inches too long. But the young man declared he couldn't care less, went to bed and fell fast asleep.

At about midnight, his sister was wide awake, worrying. So she sneaked into his room, cut three inches off the trouser legs, hemmed them up neatly and went back to bed satisfied.

At three in the morning, his mother, who hadn't slept a wink, got up, slipped into her son's room, and took three inches off the trouser legs. She hemmed them up then crept quietly back to bed again.

At six in the morning, Grandma was up bright and early; took the chance while her grandson was asleep to go quietly into his room, take three inches off the wedding trousers, and . . .

Conversion

Conversion is an initial event which must become a continuous process, not something static and frozen, but a dynamic, ongoing process.

Bishop George Appleton

Philosophers have only interpreted the world differently; the point is, however, to change it.

Karl Marx

A converted cannibal is one who, on Fridays, eats only fishermen.

Convictions

Give us clear vision that we may know where to stand and what to stand for, because unless we stand for something, we shall fall for anything.

Peter Marshall

Creation

Teacher: 'How did the universe come into being?'

Student: 'I'm terribly sorry, sir; I'm sure I did know, but I'm afraid I've forgotten.'

Teacher: 'How very unfortunate. Only two persons have ever known how the universe came into being: the Author of Nature and yourself. Now one of the two has forgotten!'

Criticism

Horse Sense

A horse can't pull while kicking,
This fact we merely mention,
And he can't kick while pulling,
Which is our chief contention.

Let us imitate the good horse,
And lead a life that's fitting;
Just pull an honest load, and then
There'll be no time for kicking.

'Christaholics'

Many Christians are only 'Christaholics' and not disciples at all. Disciples are cross-bearers; they seek Christ. Christaholics seek happiness . . . There is no automatic joy. Christ is not a happiness capsule; he is the way to the father.'

Calvin Miller

Cynicism

The cynic is one who never sees a good quality in a man, and never fails to see a bad one. He is the human owl, vigilant in darkness and blind to light, mousing for vermin and never seeing noble game. The cynic puts all human actions into two classes: openly bad and secretly bad.

Henry Ward Beecher

'To be honest, it's the finest notice board in the county. . .'

Death

I don't want to achieve immortality through my work; I want to achieve it by not dying.

Woody Allen

Obviously one isn't indestructible – quite.

Margaret Thatcher, 1988

Dr Donald Grey Barnhouse told of the occasion when his first wife had died. He was driving his children home from the funeral service. Naturally, they were overcome with grief and Dr Barnhouse was trying hard to think of some word of comfort to give them. Just then, a huge truck passed them. As it did so, it's shadow swept over the car, and as it passed on in front an idea came to him.

'Children,' he said, 'Would you rather be run over by a truck or by its shadow?' They replied, 'The shadow, of course; that can't hurt us at all.' So Dr Barnhouse then said, 'Did you know that two thousand years ago the truck of death ran over the Lord Jesus . . . in order that only its shadow might run over us?'

Denominations

A strict Baptist visiting Newmarket finds himself at the race course and, knowing that nobody knows him there, decides to have a flutter. He goes to the paddock first and is intrigued to see a Catholic priest praying in Latin over a horse. He is even more surprised when it wins. The priest prays over two or three more horses and they all win. So finally, the Baptist lays half the church funds on the horse the priest next prays over. The horse starts well but then keels over before the first fence. The Baptist is distraught and rushes to ask the priest what happened. 'Ah, that's the trouble with you Baptists,' the priest replies, 'you don't know the difference between a blessing and the last rites!'

I don't mind the walls of denominationalism, but I object to the broken glass on top!

Anglicans:	Everything is prohibited, except that which is permitted.
Baptists:	Everything is permitted, except that which is prohibited.
Methodists:	Everything is permitted, even that which is prohibited.
Brethren:	Everything is prohibited, even that which is permitted.

(Vary the labels according to preference.)

Discipleship

By blood and origin, I am all Albanian.
My citizenship is Indian.
I am a Catholic nun.
As to my calling, I belong to the whole world.
As to my heart, I belong entirely to Jesus.

Mother Teresa

Unused truth becomes as useless as an unused muscle.

A W Tozer

Dietrich Bonhoeffer, one of the Christian martyrs of Germany under the Nazis, said, 'Discipleship means allegiance to the suffering Christ.'

Great leaders have always demanded personal allegiance. King Arthur bound his knights to him by rigid vows. Garibaldi, the nineteenth-century Italian patriot, offered his followers hunger, death – and Italy's freedom. Sir Winston Churchill's stirring speech in the House of Commons on 13 May 1940, is best remembered for his dramatic words: 'I have nothing to offer but blood, toil, tears and sweat.'

Disobedience

Disobedience, as well as obedience, has the power to transform a person completely. Through disobedience in a particular decision, one can falsify the whole sequence of right thinking. The pastoral epistles talk about this a lot.

Disobedience comes in a variety of disguises: as superficial indifference or as the continuous creation of problems; as ascetic rigorism or as sectarianism; as the quest for novelty or as a philosophical restlessness. All that stuff is given a lot of weight preeminently to cover a scar in the conscience that lies hidden in the background.

Dietrich Bonhoeffer

'I'd like a suit that is appropriate for a pastor with a prosperous congregation and yet shows he is sensitive to third world issues whilst retaining authority but without too much of an American TV evangelist flavour. . .'

Dogma

Every dogma has its day.

Dreams

Some girls long for beauty
And others wish for fame;
Those that burn with ambition yearn
To carve in stone their name.

I have but one desire,
And there endeavour ends:
To get my hooks on all the books
That I have lent to friends.

Education/unemployment

What are the first words of a doctoral graduate in his
first job?
'Anything to go with the Big Mac and fries?'

Encouragement – results of

It may be that you don't like your church's minister. Well, here is a tested prescription by which you can get rid of him (or her):

1　Look him straight in the eye when he's preaching, and maybe say 'Amen' occasionally. He'll preach himself to death in a short time.

2　Start paying him whatever he's worth. Having been on starvation wages for years, he'll promptly eat himself to death.

3　Shake hands with him and tell him he's doing a good job. He'll work himself to death.

4　Rededicate your own life to God and ask the minister to give you some church work to do. Very likely he'll keel over with heart failure.

5　If all else fails, this one is certain to succeed: get your congregation to unite in prayer for him. He'll soon be so effective that some larger church will take him off your hands.

Eternity

The stars shine over the mountains,
  the stars shine over the sea.
The stars look up to the mighty God,
  the stars look down on me;
The stars shall last for a million years,
  a million years and a day.
But God and I will live and love
  when the stars have passed away.

Robert Louis Stevenson

Ethics

Twentieth-century ethics can be summed up as: Do unto others before they do you!

We have grasped the mystery of the atom but we have rejected the Sermon on the Mount. We have achieved brilliance without wisdom and power without conscience. Ours is a world of nuclear giants and ethical infants.

Joseph R Sizoo

Evangelism

A newly employed American salesman stunned his bosses with his first written report, for it demonstrated quite clearly that he was nearly illiterate. He wrote, 'I seen this outfit who aint never bought ten cents worth of nothin from us and sole them some goods. i am now going to Chicawgo.' Before they could fire him, a second report arrived and it read, 'I came to Checawgo an sole them haff a millyon.' Hesitant to dismiss the man, yet afraid of what would happen if he didn't, the sales manager transferred the problem into the President's lap.

The next day the staff were amazed to see the salesman's two reports on the bulletin board, with this memo from the President. 'We ben spendin two much time tryin to spel insted of tryin to sel. I want everybody should read these letters from Gooch, who is doin a grate job, and you should go out and do like he done!'

Doug Barnett

Existentialism

Explaining how he did so well in his philosophy exam, Woody Allen said, 'I didn't know any of the answers so I left it all blank. I got 100 per cent.'

'I'm so sorry we can't help you with the Jumble Sale leaflets
– but someone's jammed the photocopier. . .'

Experience

There are many things we need to see or experience for ourselves before really understanding them:

' "Bitzer," said Thomas Gradgrind, "your definition of a horse."

"Quadruped. Gramnivorous. Forty teeth, namely twenty-four grinders, four eye-teeth, and twelve incisive. Sheds coat in the spring; in marshy countries sheds hoofs too. Hoofs hard, but requiring to be shod with iron. Age known by marks in mouth." Thus (and much more) Bitzer.

"Now, girl number twenty," said Mr Gradgrind, "you know what a horse is." '

Charles Dickens, in 'Hard Times'

Faith

Three men were walking on a wall,
Feeling, Faith and Fact.
When Feeling got an awful fall,
Then Faith was taken back.
So close was Faith to Feeling,
That he stumbled and fell too,
But Fact remained and pulled Faith back,
And Faith brought Feeling too.

God sent sex to drive a man to marriage, ambition to drive a man to service, and fear to drive a man to faith.

Luther

Fame

If the Lord's going to raise you up, then he'll raise you up. But if he doesn't raise you up, then for God's sake don't *you* do it!

Families

'We have careful thought for the stranger
And smiles for the sometime guest
But oft for our own the bitter tone
Though we love our own the best.'

Margaret E Sangster

The little lady of the house, by way of punishment for some minor misdemeanour, was compelled to eat her dinner alone at a small table in the corner of the dining room. The rest of the family paid no attention to her until they heard her saying grace: 'I thank thee, Lord, for preparing a table before me in the presence of my enemies.'

To our forefathers, our faith was an experience.
To our fathers, our faith was an inheritance.
To us, our faith is a convenience.
To our children, our faith is a nuisance.

Praying Samuels come from praying Hannahs ... and praying leaders come from praying homes.

Edward M Bounds

Flattery

After a loquacious and flattering introduction by his host, the speaker prays, 'Lord, forgive my brother for all the wonderful but exaggerated things he said about me, and forgive me for enjoying every word.'

Forgiveness

Always forgive your enemies – nothing annoys them so much.

Oscar Wilde

Freedom

'Because of Christ, this wheelchair has become the prison that set me free.'

Joni Eareckson Tada

There are two kinds of freedom: the false, when a man is free to do what he likes; the true, when a man is free to do what he ought.

Charles Kingsley

Fulfilment

I may, I suppose, regard myself or pass for being a relatively successful man. People occasionally stare at me in the streets – that's fame. I can fairly easily earn enough to qualify for admission to the higher slopes of the Inland Revenue – that's success. Furnished with money and a little fame even the elderly, if they care to, may partake of trendy diversion – that's pleasure. It might happen once in a while that something I said or wrote was sufficiently heeded for me to persuade myself that it represented a serious impact on our time – that's fulfilment.

Yet I say to you – and I beg you to believe me – multiply these tiny triumphs by a million, add them all together, and they are nothing – less than nothing, a positive impediment – measured against one draught of that living water Christ offers to the spiritually thirsty, irrespective of who or what they are.

Malcolm Muggeridge

Giving

> Do your givin'
> While you're livin'
> Then you're knowin'
> Where it's goin'!

Gifting

A dog goes into the local Job Centre. The interviewer is a little non-plussed but eventually sends him along to a circus that is in town.

Next day the dog is back again and the Job Centre man asks how he got on at the circus. 'Oh, that was no good,' replies the dog. 'They wanted a performing dog and I'm a bricklayer.'

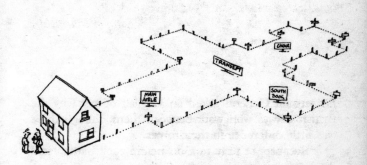

'It's a modest House Church at present – but we've got great *plans!*'

God

It is much worse to have a false idea of God than no idea at all.

Archbishop William Temple

A German General asked an English officer why the British always won wars between them, though there was little difference in their forces.

'Because we pray to God before each battle,' said the Englishman.

'But we do, too,' the General replied.

'Surely,' replied the Englishman, 'you don't expect God to understand German, do you?'

Gossip

The English preacher and teacher, Alan Redpath, described how he once formed a small group for mutual encouragement and laid down a rule that would bar gossip.

'The members subscribed to a simple formula applied before speaking of any person or subject that was perhaps controversial:

> T – Is it true?
> H – Is it helpful?
> I – Is it inspiring?
> N – Is it necessary?
> K – Is it kind?

If what I am about to say does not pass those tests, I will keep my mouth shut! And it worked!'

Alan Redpath, 'A Passion for Preaching'

Grace

A preacher's small son had to apologize for forgetting his aunt's birthday. He wrote,

'I'm sorry I forgot your birthday. I have no excuse, and it would serve me right if you forgot mine, which is next Friday.'

Heaven

A couple about to get married are killed in a car crash and end up at the Pearly Gates the day before their wedding would have taken place. They mention to St Peter that they would like a minister to marry them as soon as it was convenient. He says this will be no problem, but one hundred years later, when nothing has happened, they dare to ask him again if he could arrange the ceremony. 'I'm so sorry,' he replies, 'we're still waiting for a minister!'

Hell

Hell is oneself;
Hell is alone, the other figures in it
merely projections. There is nothing to escape
    from
And nothing to escape to. One is always alone.
                        T S Eliot, 'The Cocktail Party'

Hindrances

A hindrance is someone who gets things off to a flying stop.

Homelessness

An article in the *Independent* newspaper in December 1992 quoted the following statistics.

'More than 600 homeless people died on the streets of England and Wales [in 1991] . . . Based on coroners' records, it shows death rates among homeless people are three times higher than for the rest of the population. The homeless are also:

- 150 times more likely to be killed in an assault;

- Thirty-four times more likely to kill themselves;

- Eight times more likely to die of an accident;

- Three times more likely to die of pneumonia.

. . . The average age of death was forty-seven, compared with an average life expectancy in Britain of seventy-three for men and seventy nine for women.'

Honesty

The children in a prominent family decided to give their father a book of the family's history for a birthday present. They commissioned a professional biographer to do the work, carefully warning him of the family's 'black sheep' problem: Uncle George had been executed in the electric chair for murder. 'I can handle that situation so that there will be no embarrassment,' the biographer assured the children. 'I'll merely say that Uncle George occupied a chair of applied electronics at an important Government Institution. He was attached to his position by the strongest ties and his death came as a real shock.'

The Hollywood film director, Sam Goldwyn, said:

'I don't want any "yes-men" around me. I want men and women who tell me the truth, even if it costs them their jobs!'

It's such an honest town, Securicor uses mopeds.

Hope (false)

Probably nothing in the world arouses more false hope than the first four hours of a diet.

'Why art thou so heavy, O my soul. . .?'

Human beings

Such is the human race. Often it does seem such a pity that Noah . . . didn't miss the boat.

Mark Twain

Humility

During the prayers in the vestry before the service, the deacon prayed: 'Lord, take our preacher this evening and just blot him out.'

A Keswick speaker started his address with the comment, 'You know, you only get to speak at Keswick twice: once on your way up, and once on your way down. It's nice to be back again!'

Corrie Ten Boom was once asked if it was difficult for her to remain humble. Her reply was this:

'When Jesus rode into Jerusalem on Palm Sunday on the back of a donkey, and everyone was waving palm branches and throwing garments on the road and singing praises, do you think that for one moment it ever entered the head of that donkey that any of that was for him?'

She continued, 'If I can be the donkey on which Jesus Christ rides in his glory, I give him all the praise and all the honour.'

After a long introduction to a speaker, which listed all his outstanding achievements, the speaker stood up and said, 'I feel like the fly that hit the windscreen; I never knew I had so much in me!'

Humour

Will Rogers, the American humorist, has commented that, 'Everything is funny as long as it is happening to somebody else.'

O Lord, make my enemies ridiculous!

Voltaire

Wit is a sword; it is meant to make people feel the point as well as see it.

G K Chesterton

Hypocrisy

The Eastern European theologian, Dr Peter Kusmic, writes, 'A credible message needs a credible messenger because charisma without character is catastrophe!'

He was a good man in the worst sense of the term.

Mark Twain

There are only two things I can't stand about him: his face.

A lion met a tiger
        as they drew beside a pool.
Said the tiger, 'Tell me why
        you're roaring like a fool.'
'That's not foolish,' said the lion
        with a twinkle in his eyes.
'They call me king of all the beasts
        because I advertise!'
A rabbit heard them talking
        and ran home like a streak.
He thought he'd try the lion's plan
        but his roar was just a squeak.
A fox came to investigate –
        had luncheon in the woods;
So when you advertise, my friend
        be sure you've got the goods!

The number one cause of atheism is Christians. Those who proclaim God with their mouths and deny him with their lifestyles is what an unbelieving world finds simply unbelievable.

Karl Rahner

'Touch my board once again and I'll smash your face in!'

A vicar was asked to take the funeral for a non church-going parishioner. 'We want a nice Christian funeral,' the family said, 'but nothing religious.'

Idealism

An idealist is a man with both feet planted firmly in the air.

Franklin D Roosevelt

Identity

A group of British soldiers got lost in the desert during the Gulf Crisis. They eventually stumbled across an American Five-Star General who was surveying the field. 'Do you know where we are?' the men blurted out.

The General, very annoyed that they were improperly dressed, didn't salute or address him as 'Sir' responded with an indignant question, 'Do you know who I am?'

'Now we've got a real problem,' said one of the soldiers. 'We don't know where we are, and he doesn't know who he is!'

We have become a grandmother.

Margaret Thatcher, 4 March 1989

Incarnation

He became what we are that he might make us what he is.

Athanasius,
fourth-century theologian and apologist

Indifference

They came first for the Communists, and I didn't speak up because I wasn't a Communist. Then they came for the Jews, and I didn't speak up because I wasn't a Jew. Then they came for the Trade Unionists, and I didn't speak up because I wasn't a Trade Unionist. Then they came for the Catholics, and I didn't speak up because I was a Protestant. Then they came for me – and there was no one left to speak up for me.

Martin Niemoller,
German pastor, victim of Nazi Concentration camp

Integrity

Why is it that men know what is good but do what is bad?

Socrates

What is morally wrong can never be politically right.
Abraham Lincoln

Intelligence

He was so clever that he didn't take a book to bed with him, he just browsed through his mind for half an hour.

Douglas Adams

'This is so *exciting* – I've never done a baptism for the Mafia before!'

Involvement

Henry Dunant was born to wealthy parents in Switzerland in 1828. Deeply compassionate, he devoted considerable time to assisting and encouraging young people, especially the poor. When only about eighteen, he founded a Young Men's Christian Union.

Later, this sensitive person journeyed to Italy for an audience with Emperor Napoleon III, who was busy driving the Austrians out of Northern Italy. Arriving shortly after a horrendous battle, Henry Dunant couldn't believe what he saw. Some 40,000 men, wounded, dying and dead, lay scattered over a bloody terrain, for vermin and vultures to consume.

Forgetting his personal agenda, Dunant pitched in, doing whatever he could to help the overworked doctors. He subsequently wrote and spoke on the horrors of war. At last the Geneva Convention of 1864 convened to consider common problems. Twenty-two nations took part and signed accords acknowledging the neutrality of medical personnel in time of hostility. They chose as their banner and symbol a red cross on a white field. And so the Red Cross was born.

Joy

I have tried in my time to be a philosopher; but, I don't know how, cheerfulness was always breaking in.

Samuel Johnson

Judgementalism/jumping to conclusions

There were three zoology students, and each was sent to a different part of the world to find out about spiders.

The first was sent to Africa. After a few weeks a report arrived for his professors, saying that he'd discovered some spiders that climbed trees.

The second student was sent to South America. After a few months a posthumous report arrived saying that he'd discovered a lethal species of spider.

The third was sent to Australia. They heard not a word from him for a whole year, but then he came back in person, bringing with him a carton full of the particular species of spider that he'd been studying.

Very excitedly, he rang up his professors and got them all to meet him one morning. When they were all sitting round the table, the student put one of the spiders in the middle of it.

He looked hard at it and said, 'Walk!', and it obediently walked around the table and came back to the middle. The student said to it again, 'Walk!' and again the spider walked round the table and came back to the middle.

Then the student caught up the spider, and his professors watched aghast as he picked off its eight legs, one by one. Then he put it down again in the middle of the table.

He looked at it hard.

'Walk!' he said. Nothing happened.

'Walk!' he said again, more loudly. Still nothing happened.

'There!' he exclaimed. 'That proves my theory! Spiders without legs are deaf!'

Justice

'I'm not interested in the bloody system! Why has he no food? Why is he starving to death?'

Bob Geldof
interviewed about starvation in Africa, 1985

Learning that her husband had betrayed her, Vera Czermak jumped out of her third-story window in Prague. The Czech newspaper, *Vicerni Prahi*, reported that Mrs Czermak was recovering in hospital, after landing on her husband, who was killed.

As a boy, Woodrow Wilson worshipped his father, who was a church minister, and was overjoyed when the stern man would allow him to come along on visits through the parish.

Later, when he was President of the United States, Wilson laughingly recalled the time when his father had taken him to see a neighbour. Seeing the horse and buggy that had brought the minister and his son, the concerned neighbour wondered aloud,

'Reverend, how is it that you're so thin and gaunt, while your horse is so fat and sleek?'

The Reverend began a modest reply but before he could say two words, his outspoken son announced, to the parishioner's dismay, 'Probably because my father feeds the horse, and the congregation feeds my father.'

Knowledge

Nothing worth knowing can be understood by the mind.

Woody Allen

'You'll soon get used to this new system: just pick up the bar code reader at the end of your pew and . . .'

Leadership

Lead, follow, or get out of the way!
Ted Turner, American media mogul and owner of CNN

Leisure

Personally, I have always looked on cricket as organised loafing. *Archbishop William Temple*

Lies

No man has a memory long enough to be a successful liar. *Abraham Lincoln*

Life – living a worthwhile one

If you would not be forgotten
As soon as you're dead and rotten,
Either write things worth reading
Or do things worth the writing.
Benjamin Franklin

Life with Christ is an endless hope; without him, a hopeless end.

May you live all the days of your life.

Jonathan Swift

Listening

His thoughts were slow,
His words were few and never formed to glisten.
But he was a joy to all his friends,
You should have heard him listen!

Love

The biggest disease today is not leprosy or tuberculosis, but rather the feeling of being unwanted, uncared for and deserted by everybody. The greatest evil is the lack of love and charity.

Mother Teresa

Take away love and our earth is a tomb.

Robert Browning

The Bible tells us to love our neighbours and also to love our enemies, probably because they are generally the same people.

G K Chesterton

Media

Released in the United States in 1979 by Warner Brothers, the film *Jesus* has been dubbed into more than 130 languages and viewed in 155 countries by more than 355 million people. More than 200 mission agencies and denominations have used the film. By 1993 Campus Crusade, the catalyst for the translation effort, hopes to translate the film into all of the 271 languages spoken by more than one million people. Other organizations are interested in translating it into still more languages. Campus Crusade estimates that more than 30 million people have indicated decisions to follow Christ as a result of watching the film.

'Yes, there are quite a few House Churches on this estate...'

Television is ... a medium. So called because it is nei-
ther rare nor well done!   *Ernie Kovacs*

I find television very educating. Every time somebody
turns on the set I go into the other room and read a
book.   *Groucho Marx*

Ministers of religion

Why don't ministers look out of their windows in the
morning?

Because they'd have nothing to do in the
afternoon.

Miracles

The following story, recorded by Perrott Philips,
appeared in *Time Off* magazine.

Flying his private plane over Los Angeles, an
eighty-year old pilot had a sudden heart attack and died
at the controls. Without a moment's hesitation, the

passenger, sixty-nine year old Charles Law – who had never flown a plane before – took over the wheel of the Cessna 150 and landed it safely at Upland California. 'I don't know how he did it,' said police sergeant John Cameron, who led a convoy of ambulances and fire engines to the air strip. 'It was a miracle.'

It certainly was. After he had landed, Charles Law had to be led gently from the plane. He is blind.

Misunderstanding

A man found a penguin wandering down the street, so took hold of its flipper and found the nearest policeman. 'What shall I do with it?' he asked. The policeman thought for a moment and then suggested, 'Take it round the corner to the zoo.'

The next day the policeman bumped into the man again, who was still clutching the penguin by the flipper. Before the policeman could say anything, the man smiled and said, 'Thanks for the idea about going to the zoo yesterday. I'm taking it to the pictures today!'

A chaplain was asked to visit an oriental patient in intensive care. He soon discovered that the man didn't speak English but, as he stood and held his hand, the man constantly repeated a strange-sounding phrase. The man became more and more anguished until finally he passed away, still muttering those words.

The chaplain rang up a friend who came from the east, and asked him what the phrase meant. 'Was it some last act of repentance?' he suggested.

'No,' says the friend, 'it simply means, 'You're standing on my oxygen supply.'

A Welsh preacher worked himself into a frenzy preaching on Psalm 42, 'As the hart pants for the waterbrook so longs my soul after Thee.'

As he continued, he cried, 'Yes, brothers and sisters! It's your pants he wants!'

Money

The average English cat costs £145 per year to feed – which is more than the average income of the one billion people who live in the world's fifteen poorest nations.

The trouble is that there's always too much month left at the end of the money.

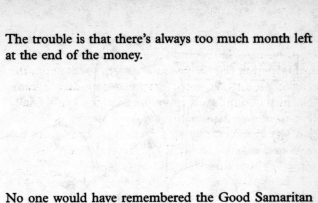

No one would have remembered the Good Samaritan if he'd only had good intentions. He had money as well.

Margaret Thatcher, speech, 1980

No man is rich enough to buy back his past.

Sometimes, when you've read through a long, spiritual prayer letter, you eventually realise that it was a veiled plea for more money. Those sorts of letters demonstrate that 'faith without hints is dead.'

'Say – could be our lucky day! The Rose window at York Minster has just fallen out!'

A pastor was driving back from a speaking engagement and decided to stop overnight in a motel. She pulled off the motorway and went into the reception area of a nice-looking motel. 'How much is a room for the night?' she asked.

'It's £110,' replied the receptionist.

'Oh. Haven't you anything cheaper?'

'Well,' said the receptionist, 'it's £110 on the first floor but it's only £100 on the second floor.'

'No, that's still too much,' said the pastor.

'The third floor is £80,' said the receptionist, helpfully.

'And what about the fourth?' asked the pastor.

'That's the top floor and that's £50 per night.'

At that the pastor turned to go. 'I'm sorry,' she said, 'your hotel just isn't tall enough for my pocket.'

New Age

I was caught cheating in a metaphysics exam. I was looking into the soul of the boy next to me.

Woody Allen

Obedience

It's hard to get your heart and your head to agree in life. In my case, they're not even friendly.

Woody Allen

Optimism

A couple have twin sons, one of whom is a pessimist and the other an optimist. The parents decide to try to even things out for their birthday, so they give the pessimist a marvellous hi-fi system. When he unwraps it, he complains, 'With the price of CDs I'll never be able to afford any! And these things are always going wrong! And you'll soon be moaning about the noise . . .'

The optimist receives just a bag of horse manure. As he unwraps it, he leaps in the air with joy, crying, 'There's a pony on its way!'

Pastors

Nehemiah was the model pastor, dealing so gently with those who let their children marry outside the faith:

'So I argued with these parents and cursed them and punched a few of them and knocked them around and pulled out their hair; and they vowed before God that they would not let their children intermarry with non-Jews.'

Nehemiah 13:25, Living Bible

The evangelist's job is to get people out of Egypt. The pastor's job is to get Egypt out of the person.

The task of pastoral ministry is, above all else, to arrange the contingencies for an encounter with the Divine.

Dietrich Bonhoeffer

Permissiveness

We cannot have permissiveness in sex and expect that we will not also have permissiveness in violence, or in tax avoidance, or corruption and bribery in high places. People today want permissiveness in the bedroom but not in the board rooms; in the casino, but not in the bank. If we promote permissiveness where we want it, we find permissiveness where we do not want it.

Sir Frederick Catherwood

Persistence

I am extraordinarily patient, provided I get my own way in the end. *Margaret Thatcher, quoted in 'The Observer', January 1983*

Personality

A well-balanced person? Someone who has a chip on both shoulders.

As the little girl prayed: 'Dear God, please make all the bad people good, and please make all the good people nice.'

'I'm sorry, I've nothing left for the 6.30pm Prayer and Praise, but I can let you have two seats behind a pillar for the 11.00am Family Worship.'

Custard Christians: those who get upset over trifles.

Yoghurt Christians: those who sour everything they mix with.

Pessimism

A pessimist is the person who looks through the obituary column in the newspaper to see if his name is there yet.

Pluralism

I think I need to pray; know any good religions?
Douglas Adams

All roads may lead to Rome but only one ends up in heaven.

Mark Green

Politically correct speak

Cerebrally non-motivated (stupid)

Chronologically gifted (old)

Differently sized (fat)

Follicularly challenged (bald)

Knowledgably dispossessed (mistaken)

Hesychastic truths perceived through ontological media (certainty)

Atonally exciting (off key)

Politics

Capitalism is man's exploitation of man, whereas communism is the exact opposite.

Pornography

At present the pornography industry in the UK is worth at least £500 million a year. In the United States it grosses more than the music and film industries combined.

Campaign Against Pornography and Censorship

Poverty

When you're down and out, something always turns up
– and it's usually the noses of your friends.

Orson Welles

Power

Of all forces, violence is the weakest.

Gobineau

Praise

Praise undeserved is satire in disguise.

Prayer

I can concentrate better when my knees are bent.

Prayer and action

A priest in a poor inner city area desperately needed money for a new church building. At his wits' end, he pleaded with God: 'Lord, if you love me, let me win the national lottery this week!' Friday was the grand draw, but there was nothing for the priest.

He went back to church to plead with God again: 'Lord, if you love me, let me win the national lottery this week!' But at the end of the week, another winner was announced.

A third time he returned to pray at the altar: 'Lord, if you love me, let me win the national lottery this week!' As he got up to go, a voice boomed from the heavens: 'OK. But meet me half-way. This week, buy a lottery ticket!'

'I sometimes think he tries a bit too hard at family services!!'

Prayers answered

I asked God for strength, that I might achieve.
I was made weak, that I might learn humbly to obey.

I asked for health, that I might do greater things.
I was given infirmity, that I might do better things.

I asked for riches, that I might be happy.
I was given poverty, that I might be wise.

I asked for power, that I might have the praise of
  men.
I was given weakness, that I might feel the need of
  God.

I asked for all things that I might enjoy life,
I was given life that I might enjoy all things.

I got nothing that I asked for – but everything that I
  had hoped for.
Almost, despite myself, my unspoken prayers were
  answered.
I am among all men, most richly blessed.

Anonymous Confederate soldier
of the American Civil War

Preachers and preaching

Some students never study but, like the spider, spin everything out from within, making beautiful webs that never last. Some are like ants that steal whatever they find, store it away, and use it later. But the bee sets the example for us all. He takes from many flowers but he makes his own honey.

Francis Bacon

My preacher's eyes I've never seen
Though the light in them may shine,
For when he prays, he closes his,
And when he preaches, I close mine.

The vicar was hoping to get a discount on the price of a suit.

'I'm just a poor preacher!' he said to the shop keeper.

'Yes, I know,' the shop keeper replied. 'I've heard you preach.'

A rather timid minister was told by one part of the congregation to preach 'the old-fashioned gospel', and by the rest to be more broadminded. One day he got up to preach and ended up saying, 'Unless you repent, in a measure, and are saved, so to speak, you are, I am sorry to say, in danger of hell-fire and damnation, to a certain extent.'

Now I lay me down to sleep:
The sermon's long and the subject deep;
If he gets through before I wake,
Someone give me a gentle shake.

On accepting his first church, a young pastor asked an elderly board member if he had any wise advice. The elderly man responded, 'Son, a sermon is like a good meal; you should end it just before we have had enough.'

Preachers can talk
But never teach
Unless they practice
What they preach.

I preached as never sure to preach again, and as a dying man to dying men.

Richard Baxter

Orators are most vehement when their cause is weak.

Cicero

On the frequent lack of application to life of the text: We often speak eloquently of the general state of the rubber industry in the West, when people simply want to know how to mend a flat tyre!

Predictability

The British won't fight.

Leopoldo Galtieri to Alexander Haig, 10 April 1982

Promises

Many people have seen the Passion Play performed in the Bavarian village of Oberammergau. It is a once-in-a-decade spectacular involving practically all 4800 villagers and much of their livestock. The 1984 presentation marked its three hundred and fiftieth staging and the eight-hour performance ran for one hundred days, beginning on 20 May.

The tradition is said to have originated in 1633 when the survival of the village was threatened by plague. Its records for 1632 reveal that at least eighty-four villagers died from plague that year, and in 1633 they sought relief by promising God that if he would turn the plague away from them they would stage, every ten years, a drama re-enacting the life and death of Christ. It is said that from that day the plague did not claim a single life in the community.

The following year, 1634, the villagers made good their promise and staged the first Passion Play.

Prophecy

H L Mencken, an American journalist covering a rather dull and, he thought, predictable Presidential convention meeting, sent the Press Release the day before. However, a crucial issue in the meeting went quite the other way from what was expected. Mencken cabled the newspaper office with the simple instruction: 'Insert "not" as sense requires.'

Purpose

God has created me
to do him some definite service.
He has committed some work to me which he has
not
committed to another.
I have my mission.
I may never know it in this life,
but I shall be told it in the next.
I am a link in a chain,
a bond of connection between persons.
He has not created me for naught;
I shall do good – I shall do his work;
I shall be an angel of peace,
a preacher of truth in my own place
while not intending it
if I do but keep his commandments.
Therefore I will trust him.
Whatever I am, I can never be thrown away.
If I am in sickness, my sickness may serve him;
in perplexity, my perplexity may serve him.
if I am in sorrow, my sorrow may serve him.
He does nothing in vain.
He knows what he is about.
He may take away my friends,
he may throw me among strangers,
he may make me feel desolate,
make my spirits sink,
hide my future from me – still
He knows what he is about.

Cardinal Newman

Quarrels

People generally quarrel because they cannot argue.
G K Chesterton

Relationships

Bakker started out loving people and using things, but then he started loving things and using people.
Jerry Miller, Prosecutor at fraud trial of Jim Bakker

Repentance

A deacon, frequently called on to pray at the church prayer meeting, always concluded his prayer, 'And now, Lord, clean all the cobwebs out of our lives.'

The others knew what he meant – all the little unsightly words, thoughts and deeds that we let accumulate in our lives. Finally it got too much for one of the brethren who had heard that prayer many times. So on hearing it again, he jumped to his feet and shouted, 'Don't do it, Lord! Kill the spider!'

Research

If you steal from one another, it's plagiarism. If you steal from many, it's research.

Salvation

Give me your tired, your poor,
Your huddled masses yearning to breathe free,
The wretched refuse of your teeming shore,
Send these, the homeless, tempest-tossed, to me:
I lift my lamp beside the golden door.

Emma Lazarus

Second Coming of Christ

I've no idea when Jesus is coming back. I'm on the Welcoming Committee, not the Planning Committee.

Tony Campolo

Secularisation

The first Law of Secularisation: 'Hollywood loves you and has a marvellous plan for your life.'

Self-pity

Self-pity is our worst enemy and, if we yield to it, we can never do anything wise in the world.

Hellen Keller

'Are you sure you are aware of the spiritual significance of baptism?!'

Sermons

A sermon doesn't have to be eternal to be immortal.

After a rather long and dull sermon the preacher asked a deacon, 'Do you think I should have put more fire in my sermon?'

'You should have put more sermon in the fire!' he replied.

Service

No matter how humble our gifts, we can use them to serve God.

In 1963 the verger at Fairford Parish Church in Gloucestershire took pity on a stray kitten. It made its home in the church where it caught mice and scared off the bats.

Tiddles was well-behaved during sermons, usually sleeping through them, curled up on the lap of one of the congregation.

When it died it was buried in the churchyard and a memorial was raised over the grave, recording seventeen years of faithful service as 'The church cat.'

I don't know what your destiny will be but one thing I know, the only ones among you who will be really happy are those who have sought and found how to serve.

Albert Schweitzer

Seven deadly sins

E Stanley Jones, an American missionary, statesman, author and lecturer, formulated what he called the seven deadly sins:

> Politics without principle,
> Wealth without work,
> Pleasure without conscience,
> Knowledge without character,
> Business without morality,
> Science without humanity,
> Worship without sacrifice.

Shared leadership

As a busy mother commented, 'It took me a lot longer to make breakfast this morning. My children helped me!'

Sincerity

It was the great Methodist evangelist, John Wesley, who told his young preachers: 'Don't worry about how to get crowds. Just get on fire and the people will come to see you burn.'

Single-mindedness

Don't grumble, don't bluster,
    don't dream and don't shirk,
Don't think of your worries,
    but think of your work.
The worries will vanish,
    the work will be done;
no man sees his shadow,
    who faces the sun.

Do all the good you can
By all the means you can
In all the ways you can
In all the places you can
At all the times you can
To all the people you can
As long as ever you can.

John Wesley

Society

In the United States of America in the 1990s, in any one day:

2795	teenage girls get pregnant
372	teenage girls miscarry
1106	teenage girls have an abortion
67	babies die before one month of life
105	children die from poverty
10	children are killed by guns
30	children are wounded by guns
135,000	children bring a gun to school
6	teenagers commit suicide
7742	teenagers become sexually active
623	teenagers get syphilis or gonorrhea
211	children are arrested for drug abuse
437	children are arrested for drinking or drunken driving
1512	children drop out of school
1849	children are abused or neglected
3288	children run away from home
1629	children are in adult jails
2556	children are born out of wedlock
2989	children see their parents divorced
34,285	people lose their jobs

We have stopped being a Christian country.
> *David Jenkins, Bishop of Durham, 1987*

Sorrow

Lessons from Sorrow

I walked a mile with Pleasure;
She chatted all the way,
But left me none the wiser
For all she had to say.

I walked a mile with Sorrow
And ne'er a word said she;
But, oh, the things I learned from her
When Sorrow walked with me.

Earth has no sorrow that heaven cannot heal.
> *Thomas Moore*

How else but through a broken heart
May Lord Christ enter in?
> *Oscar Wilde*
> *in 'The Ballad of Reading Gaol'*

Sovereignty of God

At a minister's induction, the order of service declared that the hymn before the 'Act of Induction' would be, 'Our God resigns'.

'Our father who art in heaven, hollowed be thy name . . .'

Stress

When the going gets tough,
the tough go shopping.

Leaders should always remember that,
'God loves you and everyone else
has a marvellous plan for your life!'

Success

If at first you don't succeed . . . so much for sky-diving.

Only in a dictionary does success come before work.

Success is never final, failure never fatal. It's courage that counts.

The worst that can happen to a man is to succeed before he is ready.

Martin Lloyd-Jones

When I try, I fail. When I trust, He succeeds.

Suffering

Job needed a doctor, but they sent him social workers!

The Weaver

My life is but a weaving between my Lord and me,
I cannot choose the colours he worketh steadily.
Oft times he weaveth sorrow, and I in foolish pride
Forget he sees the upper and I the underside.

Not till the loom is silent and the shuttle ceased to
  fly,
Shall God unroll the canvas and explain the reason
  why
The dark threads are as needful in the weaver's skilful
  hand,
As the threads of gold and silver, in the pattern he has
  planned.

When you struggle in the darkness, don't forget what
you heard in the light.

Sunday trading

'The merchants and tradesmen camped outside Jerusalem once or twice, but I spoke sharply to them and said, "What are you doing out here, camping round the wall? If you do this again, I will arrest you." And that was the last time they came on the Sabbath.'

Nehemiah 13:2–21, Living Bible

Tact

Tact is the art of making a point without making an enemy.

Howard W Newton

THIS MUG IS SOLD IN AID OF ST. MARY'S ROOF FUND

Teaching – importance of

One Over the Edge

'Twas a dangerous cliff, as they freely confessed,
Though to walk near its crest was so pleasant;
But over its terrible edge there had slipped
A Duke and full many a peasant.

So the people said something would have to be
  done,
But their project did not at all tally;
Some said, 'Put a fence round the edge of the cliff.'
Some said, 'An ambulance down in the valley.'

And the cry for an ambulance carried the day,
For it spread to a neighbouring city.
A fence may be useful or not, it is true,
But each heart became brim full of pity –

For those who slipped over the terrible cliff.
And the dwellers in highway and alley
Gave pounds or gave pence, not to put up a fence
But an ambulance down in the valley.

'For the cliff is all right, if you're careful,' they said,
'And if folks ever slip and are dropping,
It isn't the slipping that hurts them so much
As the shock down below when they're stopping!'

So day after day, as the mishaps occurred,
Quick forth would rescuers sally,
To pick up the victims who fell from the cliff,
With an ambulance down in the valley.

Better guard well the young than reclaim them when
   old,
For the voice of true wisdom is calling;
To rescue the fallen is good, but 'tis best
To prevent other people from falling.

Better close up the source of temptation and crime
Than deliver from dungeon and galley;
Better build a strong fence round the top of the cliff,
Than an ambulance down in the valley!

Teamwork

Fred's never been much of a sportsman. When he
played in goal at football the team called him Cinderella
because he kept missing the ball.

Temptation

It is startling to think that Satan can actually come into the heart of a man in such close touch with Jesus as Judas was. And more – he is cunningly trying to do it today. Yet he can only get in through a door opened from the inside. Every man controls the door of his own life. Satan can't get in without our help.

S D Gordon

When you flee temptation, be sure you don't leave a forwarding address!

Thinking

As long as the devil can keep us terrified of thinking, he will always limit the work of God in our souls.

Oswald Chambers

If God had meant Christians to think, he'd have given them brains.

Reading moulds thinking. As I scan my shelves I spot those books other than the Bible that have influenced my personal thought and ministry, particularly my battle not to become secularized. Unless we maintain constant companionship with Christians who direct our thinking Christianly, we easily fall prey to the spirit of the times.

Katie Wiebe

A great many people think they are thinking when they are merely rearranging their prejudices.

William James

Thoroughness

He went through it like a twelve-year-old inspecting his moustache.

Translations

On the dangers inherent in translating: One Russian interpreter didn't quite know what to make of, 'The spirit is willing but the flesh is weak,' and translated it by, 'the vodka is good but the meat is bad!'

Trust

Never trust a man who, when left alone in a room with a tea cosy, doesn't try it on.

Truth

A lie can travel halfway around the world while the truth is putting on its shoes.

Mark Twain

'Er . . . this is so embarrassing – it's stuck! !'

Values – relative and absolute

Norman was the man at the factory who sounded the hooter to say when work began and finished. Every morning as he walked past the jewellers, he set his watch by the big clock in the window. One day his watch went wrong so, on the way home from work, he took it into the jewellers for mending. Next morning he picked it up and, as he was leaving the shop, put his watch right by the big clock in the window.

'Yes, I know that's always right,' said the watchmaker. 'I set it every morning by the factory hooter.'

Vision

We think too small, like the frog at the bottom of the well. He thinks the sky is only as big as the top of the well. If he surfaced, he would have an entirely different view.

Mao Tse-Tung

Our task now is not to fix the blame for the past, but to fix the course for the future.

John F Kennedy

The man who misses all the fun
Is he who says, 'It can't be done.'
In solemn pride, he stands aloof
And greets each venture with reproof.
Had he the power, he would efface
The history of the human race.
We'd have no radio, no cars,
No streets lit by electric stars;
No telegraph, no telephone;
We'd linger in the age of stone.
The world would sleep if things were run
By folks who say, 'It can't be done.'

It is for us to pray not for tasks equal to our powers,
but for powers equal to our tasks; to go forward with a
great desire forever beating at the door of our hearts as
we travel toward our distant goal.

Helen Keller

War

I confess without shame that I am tired and sick of the war. Its glory is all moonshine. Even victory the most brilliant is over dead and mangled bodies, the anguish and lamentation of distant families crying out to me for missing sons, husbands and fathers. It is only those who have not heard the shrieks and groans of the wounded and lacerated, that clamour for more blood, more vengeance, more desolation.

William Tecumseh Sherman,
General in American Civil War

Will

The secret of an unsettled life lies too often in an unsurrendered will.

Will of God

When David Livingstone was asked if he was afraid that going into Africa would be too difficult and too dangerous, he answered, 'I am immortal until the will of God for me is accomplished.'

124

Wisdom

There had never been any argument about it: Fred was the wisest and shrewdest man in town. One day a young lad in the community questioned him about it.

'Fred, what is it that makes you so wise?' he asked.

'Good judgment,' replied Fred, readily. 'I'd say it was my good judgment.'

'And where did you get your good judgment?'

'That I got from experience.'

'Where did you get your experience?'

'From my bad judgment.'

Witness

The sixteenth-century bishop, Hugh Latimer, was one of the first preachers of social righteousness in the English-speaking world. He was imprisoned for his denunciations of social and ecclesiastical abuses. While in the Tower of London he wrote, 'Pray for me; I say, pray for me. At times I am so afraid that I could creep into a mousehole.' This was the same Latimer who later walked bravely to the stake in Oxford, saying to his companion, Nicholas Ridley, as he went, 'Play the man, Master Ridley; we shall this day light such a candle, by God's grace, in England, as I trust shall never be put out.'

Words

I try to watch the words I say,
    And keep them soft and sweet;
For I don't know from day to day,
    Which ones I'll have to eat!

Worldliness

The Christian is not ruined by living in the world but by the world living in him.

Worry

Ulcers are caused not by what you eat, but by what's eating you!

You can't change the past but you can spoil the present by worrying about the future.

When I look back on all these worries, I remember the story of the old man who said, on his deathbed, that he had a lot of trouble in his life, most of which never happened.

Sir Winston Churchill

Other titles by Stephen Gaukroger
It Makes Sense
A popular, humorous and compelling look at the reasons why it does make sense to be a Christian.

Making it Work – with Action Guide
A guide through the first months of Christian living. An action guide is included for small groups.

Word For Today series
Growing Your Gifts
2 Timothy: Ministry in today's world.

Hunger for Holiness
Malachi: A call to commitment today.

Thirsty for God
Matthew 5–7: Jesus' teaching for today.

David Cohen and Stephen Gaukroger:
How to Close your Church in a Decade
A challenge to leaders and potential leaders to look at the church's effectiveness in the 1990s.